Illustrated by Maha Younus

By Brian Johnson

Henry wakes up and climbs out of bed,
Dreams of hockey are still in his head.

He looks out his window while rubbing his eyes.
It snowed all night, what a pleasant surprise!

Henry eats breakfast in his favorite hockey sweater.
Bacon, biscuits and eggs with cheddar.

"The rink is ready," says mom.
"Dad shoveled the snow."
"Finish your breakfast - to the pond you go!"

Down the path to the pond, Henry shouts,
"Come play hockey everyone!"
Henry's sister and their friends
will enjoy a day of hockey fun!

Their skates are tied
the puck is dropped.
Around the pond
the puck is knocked.

What a way to start the day,
Henry is on a break away!

He moves to the left and the right
takes his aim and shoots the puck.

The goalie saved it just in time
with a little bit of hockey luck.

Saves are made and goals are scored.
They keep track on that old scoreboard.

Grandma and grandpa dash on by.
Bringing the smell of fresh baked pie.

Their cheeks are red and the sky is blue.
Henry's dog comes running through!

They sit on top a mound of snow.
Warming up with hot cocoa.

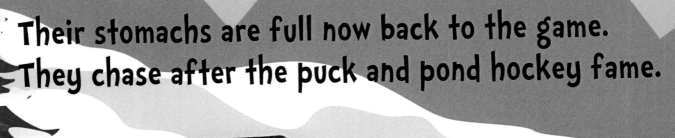

Their stomachs are full now back to the game.
They chase after the puck and pond hockey fame.

Some are fast and some are slow.
Up and down the ice they go.

The hockey flag waves in the night
as Dad turns on the hockey lights.

The game is tied the next goal wins.
Here comes Henry with turns and spins!

He shoots, he scores! They celebrate!

Towards the shore, they slowly skate.

They laugh and play around the fire.
Games and s'mores with apple cider.

It's getting late
they start to yawn.
They say goodnight
to the hockey pond.

They will come back and play again soon.
The pond glows under a full hockey moon.

Sticks and skates and hats and gloves
A day on the pond is what Henry loves.

Made in the USA
San Bernardino, CA
23 April 2018